Moments of Simplicity

Miriam Davis

ISBN 979-8-88751-763-6 (paperback)
ISBN 979-8-88751-764-3 (digital)

Christian Faith Publishing
832 Park Avenue
Meadville, PA 16335
www.christianfaithpublishing.com

All biblical citations were taken from the New International Version of the Holy Bible unless otherwise indicated.

Printed in the United States of America

To Yehoshua: My savior, my daddy, my everything.

To my daughter, Raven, who has been a guiding light and constant strength in my darkest hours.

To my grandchildren, who have done an amazing job on the cover of this book. Nana loves you. You are truly a gift.

To Mom and Pops, for the laughter, compassion, and memories. The strength I see in you is contagious. My hats off to you both.

To the ones who seem to believe there is no hope. Look up! Jesus loves you.

Come and let us return unto the Lord: For He Hath torn and He will
Heal us; He hath smitten, and He will bind us up!

—Hosea 6:1

In all things I am enriched by his grace and mercy—

Paul was called to be an apostle—not asked, no RSVPs but called.
God will use the broken, mean, angry, and hurting in such an amazing way. But sometimes it can take years for one to submit to *God's*
call. Just like in my case, I ran for years!

Remember, *God* wins every battle and is patient, but when he calls
you, *listen!*

May 13, 2022

I have been homeless,
I have been hungry,
I have been empty—
But
I pray I never experience this gift of life without forgiveness.

May 14, 2022

Lack of communication can leave you without truth.
Truth without knowledge can leave you with doubt.
Speak to the ones with true knowledge? There will be peace.

Show Your Roots

The strength of our roots can stabilize our journey if we allow our self-worth to shine through.

I should have prayed about praying,
before I prayed.

Go, then I will show.

Wind Is Picking Up

Move upon the praise of your children, Lord. Blow your presence out and over this old world today. In Jesus's name. The wind is picking up!

—<u>Newspaper</u>
June 18, 2021

Prayer

Thank you, *Lord*, for the awesome and somewhat difficult journey from the milk of your *Word* to the wisdom of your *Word*.
I have come to honor and cherish the amazing depth of your presence and peace I have found there.

—June 18, 2021

Still God

We do not get to the mountaintops alone.
We do not walk through the valleys alone.

God is still *God* in the joy,
God is still *God* in the pain.

Through the quiet unseen tears that fall,
Through the laughter of knowing his freedom.

God is still *God* in the joy,
God is still *God* in the pain.

Account

Every one of us shall give an account of himself before the *Lord*. For Christ was born, died, and rose from the grave so that He might be the Savior over the living and the dead. Give love freely, and show kindness without regret. As you breathe, share Jesus Christ with everyone you cross paths with today.

An Absolute

Anxiety is a paralyzing obstacle; a permanent acceptance of this thorn in our *side* seems like a go-to comfort these days. My level of go-to comfort ran me over last week. My fault completely. I didn't start a single day with prayer—no thankful heart, no joy. I had hope, but I didn't let it hold my hand. I couldn't go back and change my selfish attitude and couldn't explain the physical or mental consequences, but I felt them. I accept and acknowledge my shame and my lack of honor and respect for my savior, my friends, and my commitments. If I'm gonna speak it, I better live it and pray it. My choices determine my outcome. Forgiveness is a blessing, prayer is an open window, and Jesus is an *absolute*!

Sunflower Power

I love the sunflower! At a time in my life when I felt small and unworthy of love, I was out in the country, and the only thing out in the field was a nine-foot-tall sunflower. I could hardly wrap one hand around the stem of this massive flower! The face was enormous and magnetic. There was no sun out at the time, so it was bent over as if it were looking at me. Looking into the face of this beautiful creation of *God*, I felt strength begin to swell up within me. I knew at that moment I was worthy of love and accepted myself in a way I had never done before.

May 2, 2022

Love my Savior?
an absolute

Simple and outspoken?
completely

Loyal always?
pinkie promise

I Am Wanted

I am not letting go of the strength you have built within me.

I am not stepping off the path you have paved for me.

No matter what may come,
No matter what may be said.

I will trust you, Lord. You are the center of my *world*!
I am wanted.

—May 19, 2020
11:09 a.m.

God, Where Are You?

I have no strength or energy left to fight through this battle. How do I fight being invisible and empty? I hear no words from you. I do not feel your presence. I feel nothing! If I act up on my emotions, I will fail!

God, where are you?

—March 22, 2021

What Is Life?

A gift, a journey, a struggle, a victory, a lesson, an opportunity, a stage, a jar full of tears, a heartbeat, a breath, a soul, a light, a blessing?
You are life, inhale the beauty of you.

The Answer

We ask for strength and *God* gives us difficulties, which make us
strong...
We pray for wisdom and *God* sends us problems—the solution of
which develops wisdom...
We plead for prosperity and *God* gives us brain and brawn to work...
We plead for courage and *God* gives us dangers to become overcome...
We ask for favors and *God* gives us opportunities...
This is the answer.

—Newspaper

Give Up? Never

He hears me when I'm laughing.
He feels each tear that falls.
He knows my every weakness.
So he gives me *love* to make me strong.

He touches every part of my
Life with his mighty, awesome hands.
He teaches me his wisdom.
I know *God* has a plan.

So when I start to feel low and it seems that no one cares, I look up to heaven with a heavy heart. He's waiting there with outstretched arms.

—Written in the late nineties

Reality

The body must die for
the spirit to rise—

The heart must be broken
to love completely—

The soul must weep for
the joy to awaken—

Dancing Flames

As the dancing flames draw me into a hypnotic, seductive rest, within
the silence of the room, above the crackling of the wood, I hear
my mother breathing.
As I turn to look at her sleeping, reality has found me once again.

—March 22, 2022
12:45 p.m.

God allows what he hates
to draw us to his undeniable
love, mercy, and grace.
Pain, accidents, broken hearts,
suicidal thoughts, loss.
Suffering at our greatest.

Peter reminds us that we
must suffer for him as he
suffered for us.

Speak the promises,
seek his face.
Witness his vision,
see his grace.

We study the steps of Jesus.
Let's study the stops of Jesus.

Significance

Do not lose what you have going after what you want. What *God* has given you needs time to grow.
The growth is significant.

You are *priceless*.

The Sweetest Offering

When we have nothing left to give, defeated, crawling to the foot of the cross. The oils of our brokenness and tears fill the father's nostrils with such an aroma so overwhelming. He leaves his throne and comes to us. There is no greater love than the love of Jesus Christ!

—May 4, 2021

Reflection

Never underestimate the beauty within the image of your reflection through emotion.

Who Am I?

Am I a tree waiting for
my last small leaf to fall?

Am I a seed buried under
the winter snow longing to
become a beautiful rose?

Who am I?

I am a child of God!

My Blessing

Destiny falls from the sky every now and then…

Blessings fall from heaven for someone every now and again.

You know the dreams and plans I have had for me, and from your point of view, my plans just didn't fit.

So you sent me a piece of heaven in the valley I was in…

Thank you, Lord, for my beautiful blessing, Raven Michelle.

—March 1997

Help me, Lord, to find
my way to your feet
to praise your name in the
middle of my defeat.

Be my father and I will
be your child.
Hold my hand through
the hardest of miles.

Until my life's journey finds
me at your door,
And I will rest in your
Arms forevermore.

Sometimes it's not the prayers you pray that matter...
But what you learn while you wait for the answers...

Simplicity

I can honestly say I wonder how the love of *God* could save someone
like me who never really knew how to pray—
When I dropped to my knees and humbled myself in the presence
of my *God*—
The blessings flowed upon me, and now heaven is an open door.

Use Me, Lord

Lord, for the one who
experiences the loyalty I
have for you—

> Give them sight…

Lord, for the one who
acknowledges my honor for you—

> Lift them up…

Lord, for the one who comes
to realize that my tears are
a precious gift to you—

> Tear down the walls…

Lord, for the one who sees
your light shining through—

> Reveal yourself to them as
> you have me…

Dedicated to my beautiful friends
on the street and at the
homeless shelter.

Jesus loves you and so do I.

An Original

Don't allow someone's harsh *words* cause you to lose sleep.

Don't allow someone's unthoughtful actions change your mind.

Don't allow someone's lack of attention bruise your soul.

You are an original!

No another like you anywhere...

As an original, go light your world!

Give Christ

How many people do you know of that will show up at a church for
    a free meal and leave with Christ in his heart and joy from his
    mouth?
Christ says: "Come for my blessing and mercy."
Free food opens doors to deliverance—

(worked with homeless in past summers)

Strength

Strength to the people who have allowed the tears to fall—
Praise for the storms conquered that help us reach the foot of the
cross.

I am nothing without Jesus Christ.

Grant that I may seek—

Rather to comfort than be comforted.

To understand than to be understood.

Rather to love than to be loved.

For it is by self-forgetting that one finds.

It is by forgiving that one is forgiven.

For it is by dying that one awakens to eternal life.

Amen—so be it, *Lord*.

Love Like Jesus—

No regret, hesitation, anger, judgment, or question.

Love Like Jesus—

The beauty of a mother's love compares to no other.
The tears, anger, loss, disbeliefs, and misunderstandings
All fall away when wrapped in her arms.
I love and honor you Mama.
You are living proof of what beauty truly is.

(also one of my *card* designs)

Mother's Day 2022

Happy

Mercy is a gift, pass it on.

I will not silence my joy for anger.

No one can steal "my happy" that God himself has given me!

I have a hope beyond the undertaker.

Jesus says, "Drink from the brook and I will do the rest."
As we seek out the light the darkness gathers.

Do not cry out in fear but in hope and in faith.

Shine in your world today,
In Jesus's name.

God is my creator—

My daughter is my hero—

My grandbabies are treasures from heavens vault—

March 16, 2021
6:00 a.m.

May you be happy
May you be blessed
May you be healthy
May you be safe

God keep you today.

—Newspaper

When God sends someone in need your way for food, shelter, cloth-
ing, prayer, encouragement,
Do not base your decision through worldly advice or human
observation

But in prayer alone—

You may be entertaining angels.

(Written and sent to a pastor who refused to help me and my dog in
our time of need)

Why?

Why must I ask you to be my friend?
Why must you always turn away?
This life is full of pain, too much to understand.

You look at me as if I am nothing.
I am a person with dreams, thoughts, and prayers.
A beautiful gift of life just as you.
True to what I must become.
Take my hand and I will be your friend.

I am loved by *God* and I never walk alone.
My story is not over, it is just beginning.
There is a purpose that is bigger.
There is a plan that is better.

The Shepherd

When one lost sheep dies to the brokenness of this sinful life and finally finds his way

When one lost sheep dies to the tears and sorrow that bring loneliness and pain

When one lost sheep dies

The shepherd smiles.

Struggle of the Seeds

Absolutely a seed no one
wanted and still don't want.
But I will stretch toward
the heavens and shine.
My petals have been broken,
my seeds scattered in hopes,
they fall through the cracks and never take root.
Well, *God* chose different!
My roots are strong, my
growth continuing, and the
colors of myself outshine
the darkness you wanted
for me. I'm here, I'm
beautiful, and I'm not
going anywhere.

An Afternoon Prayer

Lord, for the times I forget how to be happy and remember your blessings. Bring good memories and thoughts to my mind. Show me your goodness and give me a heart of joy once again. Thank you, Father. Amen

My life is full of gifts blessings and joy.
I am *not* a victim. I am an empowered overcomer.
I am worth my own self-love and self-acceptance.
I am not a burden when I ask for help and support.
I am creating my life, not reacting to it.
I am responsible and accountable for my actions and choices.
I will succeed in this world.

I am *loved*
by Jesus Christ.

—Newspaper

Don't let people tell you what to believe.

Strong holds demand thinking.

Leave what *God* tells you to leave.

God is a *God* of hearts.

Go somewhere you can grow.

Don't be a living dead Christian.

Leave and be blessed or stay and continue the mess.

Get around positive people.

Abraham had to change his environment.

—Newspaper

Truth

Christian—A word found in any part of the world and in any dictionary.

Love—Giving up one's selfish wants for another in need.

Jesus Christ—The one true reality.

Home

My love will shine through the night like a beacon guiding you home—

Home

Where our past is put away—remembered. Our present is cherished, and the future is placed in our hands, with *God* by our side, for us to mold.

Be Yourself

Let them judge you,
Let them misunderstand you,
Let them gossip about you—
Their opinions are not your problem.
You stay kind—
Committed to love and free in your authenticity…
No matter what one says or does, don't you dare doubt your worth or
the beauty of your truth…
Just keep shining like you do…

Be yourself

My Child

To my child who loves me and needs me every day—
I am always there.

To my child who often cries and no one sees the pain on their face—
Father, remind them,
I am always there.

To my child who feels rejected and doesn't understand why no one
    cares—
I am always there.

To my child who is always lonely and seems so full of fear—
Father, please remind them,
I am always there.

To my child, a single mother, who doesn't know where the next meal
    will come from—
Because of her dedication,
Father, remind her that my promises will come.

To the divorced son of mine with children to support,
Please remind him, Father,
I hear his heart.

To all my children out there who struggle to exist, provide, breathe—
Father, please remind them,
Soon, they will be coming home to live with me…

Be Still and Know

At times I have become psychologically overwhelmed by what other human beings think of me. But on my journey called life, I also discovered what it truly means to be human in *God's* eyes. Why the flaws? Why the bad choices? Why the wrong peeps? Why the extreme, emotional roller coaster? Why all the arguments with my Creator? Then one day, believe me, or not, *God* spoke to me. All he said was, "Be still and know." I was awakened. My heart began to beat again. Now I feel every emotion in intensity. I see myself and others in a way I feel he sees us. I am loved, blessed, held, treasured, and cherished. I need no church, no preacher, no family member, no friend, or no enemy to validate who I am in God's eyes. We all fall short, get too busy, worship, and idealize the wrong thing. Get off the emotional roller coaster and look up! God is the only true love that will ever stick around when no one else will. I love you, *Lord*, and I am not ashamed of you. Your love for me is priceless!

Amen?

Until I learn through *God's* grace how to rule my own mouth, mind, and heart, I will never truly enjoy the blessings of the *Lord*.

Amen?

Daddy Jesus

You are the only Father I know. What I know of you I find, I am more precious than silver or gold.

You love me from a distance yet still hold me in your arms. You help Mom sing me lullabies while angels rock me to the place of dreamer's charms.

You see my needs, my wants, my tears, and with constant care, you show me how special your love really is.

I play, I laugh, I sing my songs—"Itsy Bitsy Spider," "Old MacDonald," and "Jesus Loves Me This I Know"—all the time protecting me as down my path I go.

I've grown so fast, and yet I see the love Daddy Jesus has for me is only something I can conceive.

You brought me into this world my innocence at its best—all the while knowing that it was mommy we would bless.

So thank you, *God*, for giving me a father who will never leave and blessing mommy with a treasure blessed that only a heavenly Father can receive.

I love you, Daddy Jesus. I love you with all my heart. And when we finally meet face-to-face, from then on, I know we will never part.

Happy Father's Day

—Baby Raven
June 18, 1999

There Once Was a Man

There once was a man who walked many miles way back when
They threw a cross upon his back—
Little did they know to save the souls of man.

He carried it, he dragged it, he pulled it along
They whipped him, they kicked him, then sang out this song.

Where is your *God* with his power and might
You say you came from heaven, so come down and fight.

Nails through his hands and nails through his feet,
his earthly mother's tears and prayers fell with much defeat.

He died on the cross and suffered such pain.
But *God* knew the plan and his only son was slain.

In the end he triumphed over death and the grave.
Now through and from his blood we can be saved.

—Written 1998

Life Loved

Springtime flowers,
The smell of morning showers.

The kiss of an innocent child,
A walk on a warm summer day.

A winter wedding,
A brand-new puppy.

That's life *loved*

A mother's laughter filling the house.
A father mowing the yard.

To weep when a friend is sad.
To sincerely pray when one is ill.

To watch a family grow in pure honest love.
To watch a *loved* one's journey lead him to the crown of life.

That's life *loved*

To hear the angels sing, "Welcome home."
Jesus's hands outstretched saying, "Well done."

That's life *loved*

—Written for Doug Phillips when his father passed away
—Newspaper
Written June 24, 1999

Beauty of a Soul

The beauty of one's soul is not revealed by the surroundings of a worldly plain.

The beauty of one's soul is found in the mention of Jesus's name.

Compassion for the lost
healing for the pain
chains being broken
hearts being changed.

Tears being seen in quiet places
st rongholds being torn down
the sacrifice of our dear Savior
being spoken to one who is lost.

That is the beauty of a soul

—Written for and dedicated to Ron and Trish Davis
See you both when I get there!
Written February 2, 2020

He Will Make a Way

As I look back on my life,
questions fill my mind.
Why would such a great love
Save me? Jesus—*God's*
sacrificed one.

He shed his blood, he took
the nails while people spat on him.
The angels cried, the people
mocked, the earth began to shake.

On the cross he struggled
to breathe, to live, to cry
and not once did he say
"Father, save me!" for he
knew he had to die.

He died for you, he died for me,
so life we could obtain.
And when I look upon his nail
scarred hands and feet, this
great love will be explained.

So as we walk through
life's journey moving forward on our way,
We sometimes find ourselves looking
back on mistakes we have made.

If we keep our eyes on Jesus
and the crown of life, we will win.

We will see the problems of
this life so very small when
we come face-to-face with him.

So when you become discouraged
and troubles cloud your way—
Remember the gifts *God* has given you
And be secure in knowing that
He will make a way.

Shine

May the blessing of his light
be upon you.
Light on the inside,
Light on the outside.

May the love of the *Lord* shine
from your eyes like a candle
in a window welcoming the
weary traveler home.

May you understand the strength
and power of *God* in the
battles that approach as
a thunderstorm in winter.

And in the quiet beauty of
creation in the calm of
a summer sunset.

May you come to realize that
insignificant as you may seem
in this great universe. You
are an important part of *God's*
plan.

May he watch over you
and keep you safe from
harm.

—Written for my neighbor at the time, Jeannie
2020

He Loves Me

When my heart is sad and full of grief—
He holds me

When I'm on my knees torn and confused—
He comforts me

When my body is tired and my spirit is weak—
He brings me peace

When family and friends fail to see the path I have chosen—
He shows me forgiveness

When alone with shame, I hold death in one hand and life in the other—
He assures me I am his

When I feel rejected on my face in front of *God*—
He wraps his arms around me and lets me know he sees my heart

Why?

Because he loves me

Daddy's Presence

In my complete human loneliness, I ask *God*, "Why?"
With tears streaming down my face, within the emptiness and mis-
    understanding of my human loneliness, I cry out again, "Why?"
He whispers, "Daughter, I need your full attention."
As I look back on all the beautiful words *God* has allowed me to put
    to paper, I now understand.
I do not know of the ones who have been touched by my writings,
    but God—in these moments of my human loneliness has come
    to my room—filled my surroundings with songs of praise from
    the birds outside my open window.
As the breeze sways the curtains, I breathe in the fresh air. The whys
    disappear, my heart fills with joy, and my daddy's presence is
    another morning. Thank you, Daddy.

We are never alone.

—March 13, 2021

True Friend

Friends will let you down, loved ones say goodbye
It's hard to understand the way things work in this life
A kind heart is hard to find. The instant you feel lonely, the moment
    you feel pain

Remember

As long as you have Jesus, you will always have a friend.

To find a little peace of mind, we fill our lives with empty things—a new house, a new car, relationships that only bring pain—and at the end of life's journey, what will it all mean?

As long as you have Jesus, you will always have a friend.

—Written February 13, 2002

God's Husband for Me

To the one who will love me
I don't know who you are.
I know you're out there
faithfully waiting,
Please don't go too far.

To the one who will love me,
To the one who will share my life,
I pray for you every day
God has chosen me to be
your wife.

To the one who will love me,
and accept my child as own,
We will love with patience and
honesty and our house will
be *God's* home.

We will raise our child within
the purity of our *Lord*
Jesus Christ.
And know in precious humility
that we are doing what is
right.

In *God's* name we will move
mountains
And raise 'our' child in
love. We may feel the
sting of the desert sun

on our faces, and in *God's*
grace, we will overcome.

As our lives proceed with
God's hands on the wheel,
We will grow to experience
the true meaning of *love*
and the gift of *God's*
perfect will.

—Written November 20, 2001

All He Had

As he sat there in the crowd that day watching as the people passed
    his way.
He noticed the little woman place her small blessings in the tray.
As his heart filled with sadness for he knew what was meant to be
He told his disciples,
Look she gave everything.

She gave all she had, no name or glory did she claim.
With her two small coins, full of humbleness and praise, she placed
    them in the tray.

As he hung there on the cross that day gasping for his breath. Blood
    was streaming down his face as he looked across the crowd. He
    saw faces full of hate and felt their hearts full of sin.

He cried, "Father, to save them, I will give all I have."
He gave all he had, the Son of God he did claim.
With nails in his hands and feet, he came to save us from our sins.

With his blood falling to the ground, he came to set us free—
He was *God's* only Son,

He gave everything
Will we?

A Life Pleasing to God

What I believe about *God* affects what people believe about me. In my world, Jesus Christ is the Lord of lords and King of kings. I believe in whom Jesus Christ says he is—the truth, the life, and the only way to God our Father. My church is the world around me. Where is your church? Do your beliefs and lifestyles as a Christian sit stale on the church pew when you leave on Sunday mornings? Or do you take Jesus to the lost, abandoned, and abused on the streets? Put down the remote and dust off your Bibles! The laziness has got to stop. Fear is no excuse. Are you tired? We all are. *God* is calling us to rise up and go rescue in his name. On the day of judgment, where will you stand? World theology or *God* theology? There will be eternal consequences! I challenge you today. Lead a life that will be pleasing to *God*. Then and only then will he use you to reach this lost and dying *world*, not for your benefit and glory but for his alone.

—Written during the first six months of COVID-19
Newspaper article

Never Assume

Sunday morning…

Church day at the Home for Children. It was a very cold winter morning, with two to three feet of snow on the ground (maybe even more than that). I couldn't remember much about that day (except for the fried chicken waiting for me at lunch), but I would never forget what I witnessed at church—the way the church was set up, the overflow seating was on either side of the pulpit. Where my cottage sat, I could see the overflow section to my right. The pastor at the time was Brother Thorinton, and the superintendent of the Home for Children at that time was Brother Brown.

In any given service, Brother Brown would sit behind the pulpit to my right of the pastor. At some point during the service, the door to the overflow section opened, and an old man came in and sat down. He was wearing dirty, ragged clothes, with no coat, hat, or gloves on. It was so very cold outside, and because of his appearance, I *assumed* he was homeless and wanted and needed to get warm for a bit. What better place to do that than a church, right? The moment Brother Brown noticed the old man, he stood up, walked off the stage over to him, knelt down, and spoke something into his ear. In my mind I *assumed* he was offering a coat, a meal, or a prayer. While this scene was unfolding before me, the pastor never stopped preaching, never even turning his head to acknowledge the old man. After all this took place, the old man ran out of the church back into the cold. The superintendent took his place, seated behind the pastor. At that young age witnessing what just took place, I remembered thinking at that moment that if that was what God's love was about, I didn't want it. That old man could have been an angel. I *assumed* he was just looking to get warm and be shown some love and mercy. Instead, he was thrown out like trash.

The church no longer stands, and I believe that all involved in this traumatic event have all passed except for me. For some reason, this memory still haunts me today. So as we walk and talk with God on a daily basis, never *assume* you know the strangers or their needs he places in your path. Just open your hearts, hands, and minds to them. Share and show them his love. It's that simple, really.

Craving of a Needle

I couldn't remember dates, times, or days, but I could remember just turning eighteen years of age. I could remember just in recent days signing myself out of the Home for Children in Sevierville, Tennessee. I had moved in with a friend from high school and her family, who lived in the Wears Valley area. During my first week with her, I remembered her introducing me to a man who was a friend of the family. Later I did realize that he was a very popular drug dealer in that area. Me being unaware of who I was or where I belonged and because of the attention he showed me, we started dating. At that time I had no idea what that meant. So I started having sex with him and took part in every single drug he offered. Within my lack of knowledge, I believed that my actions were the definition of love. Boy, did I have a lot to learn! Anyway, one day my friend and I went over to visit my boyfriend and partake in the party pill of the day. Whatever drug he had, we wanted a taste of it. When we arrived, we found him out of his mind and shooting a loaded pistol out the back door of the trailer. His sister, who lived there with him, informed us he had been shooting up dope most of the day. When he realized we were there, he came into the kitchen telling us he was shooting at the men in black that had been watching him all night. I was so naive and still a virgin in every aspect of my mental thinking that when he asked if I wanted to experience the needle ride, I said yes. Okay listen, you put enough dope in a pipe, a needle, or up your nose, and you can't remember how long you have gone without sleep, a bath, or food? The devil will come to you, speak to you, and show you things—evil things! Even after witnessing the paranoia, sweating, and uncontrollable shaking from this man, believe it or not, I still wanted to experience the ride. I wanted to put that needle in my arm and see for myself. Crazy? No—just without knowledge and absolutely no self-worth. He finally laid the gun down on a table and decided to tell me he wanted another shot of "craziness" shot up his veins. *Wow!*

As I followed him down the hall to the bathroom, I asked if I could go first. He was delirious with the craving and said that if he went first, I could tie the rubber band around his arm. So I hopped up on the sink with anticipation coursing through my body, just like a child waiting in line to ride the next pony at the fair. Looking back now, I could remember it all in slow motion. I watched as he put the needle in his vein and released the dope, and before I even got the rubber band lose, he turned gray, his eyes rolled back in his head, and he fell dead on the floor right before me. I believe I was in shock and a little pissed off because I didn't get mine! As this chaos unfolded, his brother-in-law dragged his body into the hallway and began CPR. As for me, I ran out of the house, never looked back, and never went back. I was informed later that he *survived*, but for how long? Who knows. In all the fear, chaos, and slow motion of the reality of what just happened? I saw God's mercy and sacrifice for a sinful life. I just didn't understand it yet.

Years have come and gone since that day. And I admit I did eventually try the needle ride! I'm not proud of that time in my life, but because of my sinful life's journey, I met Jesus face-to-face in my deepest sorrow and pain. He left heaven to come to earth and pulled me out of my darkest darkness! I believe my complete surrender of control and of my me, me, me attitude has finally led me to a place in him where my father is proud of me. There is no better drink or drug than the precious deliverance of Jesus Christ.

Mr. Teddy

Yes, I'm not ashamed! I am a forty-seven-year-old woman who sleeps with a teddy bear. His name is Mr. Teddy! When my daughter Raven Michelle was four years of age, I was struggling as a single mom. So at Christmastime, I decided to put her name on the Angel tree at church. As they handed out the gifts after church one morning, I cried. Raven had been blessed. The only gift that wasn't wrapped was a brown bear with a red bow tie. She fell in love with him on sight! From that day on, they were inseparable. She adored, played, talked, and carried that bear everywhere! She would even dress him in her old baby clothes. Mr. Teddy went through the flu, lice, playdates, sleepovers, and trips to the market and even enjoyed hanging out with Raven on her bike and skateboard. That little bear was washed as much as she was. When Raven turned twelve years of age, she came to me with Mr. Teddy in her arms. She proceeded to inform me that she was now too old to sleep or hang out with him any longer. My heart was now broken, both in a good way and a bad. Raven was now starting to come into her own. Yes, I felt sad for Mr. Teddy and for me. My little girl was growing up. Instead of placing him in a closet or toy chest, and since Raven was too old to sleep with him or me any longer. I decided to ask her if I could sleep with him. She giggled at my question and replied that I was way too old to sleep with him. But she agreed because she knew I loved him as well.

It truly would be a sad day to watch your child, as a parent, lose interest in their special toys. It would also be beautiful to watch them grow and blossom into the person *God* created them to become. I slept with Mr. Teddy for years! He was a soothing presence to have around when Raven was no longer home. I would talk to him, cry on him, and slobber on him, and not once did he complain. I would often clutch him close and think of my baby girl all grown up and out in the world. Raven came to a crossroads in her life where she felt she no longer needed me, but I believe we all experience that age when we assume we know it all and can do life on our own. All my prayers were answered, and with the grace that *God* showed me raising her, she managed to find the man he made just for her. Mr. Teddy filled a void in my life that every parent lives through from a child's adolescent years to adulthood.

My daughter is now married living within the moments of adolescence, questions, and priceless memories of her own children. As for Mr. Teddy, yes, he's still in the family—stains and all! He was passed on to my youngest grandson and continues to be loved and cherished.

As we love and hold dear to our memories, children, and grandchildren,

Remember, for *God* so loved the world that he gave his *only Son.* Not because he had to but because his *love* for us is continuously unconditional. Just like an old-aged stained teddy bear.

Priceless.

—Started 2014
Completed December 23, 2021

The Beating of the Rocks

When the waves come pouring over the rocks in unison with a voice that will stop you in your tracks, longing to crush the empty hole below it, and as the piercing waters beat the unmovable rocks below, the water becomes clear. Never forget that within the pounding energy of the rocks from the waters above, the surface, beaten smooth and unbreakable, come forth peace and tranquility. So do you trust the breaking of the waters or the calm mirror images within the beauty of the stillness? Strength comes to us in many different ways. And I believe if not for the steady, never-ending beating of the rocks, there would be no calm mirror image to be seen.

—Dedicated and written for my sisters, Beverly and Sheila
The strength and courage you have shown
through your battles have given me hope.
February 9, 2022

Thoughts with God

Early morning sitting at my kitchen table having coffee and talking to my cats, Tabbie and Chunk. Tabbie was asleep in the chair next to me while Chunk was running around the table at my feet. Chunk decided to jump up on the chair Tabbie was sleeping in and proceeded to try and wake her up. I just smiled drinking my coffee and enjoying the silence within the house. Chunk continued to try and wake Tabbie. It seemed to me that he wanted her full attention. I thought back to a time when I allowed the devil to fill my head with lies that I was unwanted and unloved. With my history? As far as me destroying myself physically, mentally, and spiritually? I was so adolescent in my maturity and thinking—I craved attention. I would go after it like a lioness on the hunt. I didn't care where or with whom I received it from. Looking back over at Chunk going crazy trying to wake Tabbie up, needing and wanting her full attention, Tabbie just continued to sleep. In those moments, I heard *God* speak to me and say, "Just be still, keep your eyes on me, and I will give you all the attention you will ever need or want." Reading what I just wrote, I'm in the humblest of places! I have never been here before! Thank you, *Lord*, for remembering me and pulling me back to reality. I am nothing without you! I have learned the hard way that the more you pull away from *God*, the bigger the struggle. Fall into his arms and experience his one-on-one attention. I promise you, you will never be the same!

—Written: November 10, 2015
9:58 a.m.

To Love a Stranger

I have no memories of my mom holding me as a child, but now I have memories of her and I dancing in the early morning making breakfast. In her mind, she's completely unaware of who I am. Me? I know absolutely nothing of her except her giving birth to me. As with any individual suffering from dementia, I truly believe she can see her protector. Each and every one of us has an angel chosen by God to protect and watch over us always. Before we took our first breath of life, they were already with us. Mom can see hers now. She speaks of heaven a lot; now her mind is clear no more.

Mistakes forgiven, anger lay down from my past, and time spent here. The numbness is gone, and love and pity are all I seem to feel for her. I have hope praying for real decisions to be made on her behalf. But like the flowing of the rivers, time stops for no one. Neither does dementia. Sitting with her at times, she has moments of beautiful smiles and giggles. *God* showed us a little compassion today as I was able to get Mom out for a brief walk, just around the driveway in between the cars, but hey, it was good. She was holding on to my hand so tightly, and as I looked down, our feet were in unison. At that moment in my spirit, I heard, "You have not walked her path, but you are on in the same." Some lessons I have learned by being here are

> Laugh a lot.
> Pray for patience.
> Lock the door when in the bathroom.
> Hold them tight when you can.
> No matter the battle within, *never lose your faith!*

Just as the woman with the issue of blood, she reached out in faith and was healed. So as I pray to the heavens for Mom, I understand with or without healing. There are more lessons to learn and priceless memories to capture. I know what dementia is and what it does to the brain. I have been angry, felt pity, laughed, cried, screamed, and even panicked at times. This is not a job; this is Mom. This fact makes it very personal, making me protective, defensive, and a bit crazy. There have been moments in the past—remembrance on her face—a memory she doesn't share, like a soft wind blowing through her hair then it's gone. Another lesson I believe I am learning is the true definition of *love*, putting one's life on hold—plans, dreams, open doors, to be there and witness just how precious the ones God has given to us. Strength, peace, courage, and guidance to everyone who has been on a journey with loved ones and dementia.

Within my strength and compassion, I tip my hat to you.

—Written March 2022

Spirit, Ignite

As tears run down my face with such burning of neglect, I ask *God* to renew my hope and my raging voice please be taken away. As anger courses through my veins for the ones who lie and deceive, I ask my spirit to ignite with such a flame of love and for peace to flow my way.

—2021

Simple Papa

The struggles we go through,
the pain that we feel.
I'm glad *God* chose to bless
me with a daddy's love
that is real.

When I want to leave with
no peace in my mind,
My spirit torn down, my
body moving like a wheel.

After all these years, my
tears compare nothing to yours.

I honor you today with
a skip and a song.
From a little child who
would have never known.

Happy Father's Day, Pops!

—Written Father's Day 2022

A Calling

Paul was called to be an apostle, not asked, not RSVP'd but called. *God* can and will use the broken, angry, and hurting in such an amazing way, but sometimes it takes years for one used and abused to submit to God's call. *God* wins every battle and is patient to wait at times. To put off the drawing near and calling of our *Lord* and Savior, for our timing, there will be missed blessings, no open doors, hearts missed out on healing, and unbelievable sacrifices on our part. When Jesus calls, listen.

In all things, I am enriched by his grace and mercy.

—2020

As I look around the workshop,
I see the hearts' content.
They work for little pay,
but their joy is never spent.

We "normal people" take so
much for granted,
Yet they don't know what that is.
All they see is companionship
while earning money ready spent.

Spent on buying candy or
gifts for special friends,
or even brand-new tennis
shoes, or dinner at day's end.

They do not know what
selfishness or hatred truly is.
They just want to come to work,
The word that lights the spark.

The *Lord* has something
precious for these lost little lambs.
Something so wonderful
that "normal" does not compare.
And
When we get to heaven and
see these amazing souls,
We won't see the limps,

the distraught faces, or
voices never heard.

We will see the life
of Jesus shining in their eyes
As through the gates of
Glory go forever to abide.

So when you think life's
problems are far more than
you can bear,
Just come to work with
me one day, and I'll show
you faces of joy beyond compare.

—June 21, 1999

The Awakening

A little while ago, I was outside watering and bracing the sunflowers to stretch toward the heavens. Mom and Pops were outside cutting and stacking wood, staying physical, and getting exercise.

As I was standing there in my own little world, working with the flowers, I heard a mighty rushing wind behind me that caught my attention. I turned around, but the bushes near me were not moved by what I was hearing. As the rush of wind came once again, I looked up. The top of the trees was swaying in unison with such force as if someone were caressing the leaves and branches with their hands.

It was a beautiful experience of remembrance of how *God* will use his creation to get my attention. As the breeze filtered down between the tightly knit trees, it brushed across my face with such a gentle welcoming softness. And at that moment that God made it just for me, I knew all was well with my soul.

There is a beautiful awakening coming for the hearts, souls, and bodies that love him. Keep believing! Home is just in view.

—Written Wednesday, July 20, 2022

Pitiful Patty

On our journey in life, we experience many different personalities—some shy, some well-spoken, some snooty as hell. And then there are the ones with the empty eyes and a demon at the wheel, with sweet smiles, constantly watching and waiting to destroy you within your own weaknesses with their hand out. No self-esteem, way too entitled to work or support themselves. They actually abuse the help that the government supplies for them. Yes, I am speaking of a personal encounter with a Pitiful Patty, who absolutely cannot love anyone unless me, me, me is pleased, pleased, pleased.

Severe victim mentality with an arrogance of an aroma, which smells like a rich fertilizer straight from the barn. We humble folk ask our maker why? The cross was for us all. So if you're reading this out there and feel entitled, I hope your knees are sore from kneeling before the Savior. Being proud, deceitful, and empty is a surefire way to remind you that your final destination will be hot and very unpleasant. The Holy Spirit warned me of this individual many, many times. So because I wouldn't listen, Pitiful Patty revealed to me one more time that evil does walk among us. We are not here to save anyone. We can't even save ourselves. Since the cross of Calvary opened our eyes to experience a sacrifice that we are so unworthy of, now we have no barriers between us and our Creator. Memories are forever in the heart and mind, and anger must be surrendered. Forgiveness must happen. I truly wish I could reveal the true name of my Pitiful Patty, but I must love always with the love of Jesus Christ.

We were created to be loved, dream, experience, and enjoy the path and journey hand in hand with God, making his visions for our lives come to life. I will not look back, but I will kick down your pedestal, help you off the floor, and keep going. There will always be Pitiful Patties but walk away. Three is a crowd, and pitiful is Pattie's best friend. God has given new mercy every morning—a beautiful world to admire and enjoy and others to cherish. If the pure in the heart allows the darkness of this world to outshine the resurrection of God's Son, well, then, we deserve what we get. Jesus died for us, so we must rise for him. Pray for the Pitiful Patties in your world and listen to God's voice.

My repetitious ignorance stops here.

Love like Jesus did, and when the spirit speaks, try listening.

And the greatest of these is *love*.

—Written Tuesday
July 19, 2022

About the Author

Miriam Michelle Davis and her older siblings were raised in Sevierville, Tennessee, by individuals chosen by God to guide them, nurture them, protect them, and show them the love of Jesus. She is a woman built from strength, vitality, battle scars, and victories. She loves Yehoshua and has a loud, contagious laughter infectious to anyone around her. She is honored, blessed, and humbled to share her *Moments of Simplicity* with you.